Camping with Dad

Written by Jill Eggleton
Illustrated by Raymond McGrath

T0362787

2

Dad and the kids
were going camping.
They put the tent and
their sleeping bags in the truck.

Dad looked at his list.
"We have everything," he said.
"Let's go."

3

Dad loved going camping.
He was singing so loudly that
the kids put on their headphones.

"Dad is singing like a sick rhino,"
they said.
But Dad didn't care.
He just went on singing.

The truck went bumping
down the road . . .

bump, bump, bump.

Dad stopped the truck under a tree.
"This is a good place for the tent,"
he said.
But when he went to get the tent,
it wasn't on the truck.

"It must have fallen off," said Dad.
"We'll have to go back
and look for it."

Dad and the kids found the tent
lying on the road. They took it
back to the tree.

But when they looked in the bag,
there were no pegs.
"The pegs must have
fallen out," said Dad.
"It is too dark to look for them now.
We'll just have to use sticks."

The kids got some sticks
and they put up the tent.

"Now," said Dad,
"we can get into our sleeping bags."

But they didn't have any sleeping bags. "The sleeping bags must have fallen off, **too!**" said Dad.

Dad got some old sacks
from the truck.
"We can sleep in these," he said.

What a noise!

The old sacks had a **horrible** smell,
but Dad didn't care.
He went to sleep and started to snore.
"He's **snoring** like a sick rhino now,"
said the kids.

The kids went to sleep
with towels over their faces
and headphones on their ears.

But in the night, a big wind
woke up the kids.
The sticks came out of the tent
and away it went —
up into the air like a giant bird.

Instructions:
How to Put Up a Tent

You will need:

pegs

pole

tent

hammer

1

- Find a good place to put up the tent.

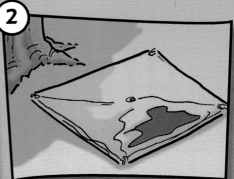

2

- Put the tent on the ground.

- Put a peg in the hole at each corner of the tent.

- Hammer the tent pegs into the ground.

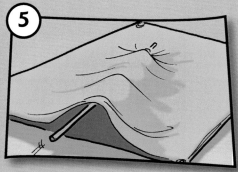

- Put the pole in the hole in the middle of the tent.

- Lift the tent up.

- Pull the ropes tight and attach them to some pegs.

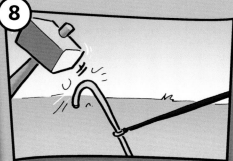

- Hammer the pegs into the ground.

Guide Notes

Title: Camping with Dad
Stage: Launching Fluency – Orange

Genre: Fiction
Approach: Guided Reading
Processes: Thinking Critically, Exploring Language, Processing Information
Written and Visual Focus: Instructions, Speech Bubbles
Word Count: 317

THINKING CRITICALLY
(sample questions)
- What do you think this story could be about? Look at the title and discuss.
- Look at the cover. Do you think Dad has been camping before? Why do you think that?
- Look at pages 2 and 3. Dad had a list. What do you think he was using the list for?
- Look at pages 4 and 5. Why do you think Dad loved going camping?
- Look at pages 8 and 9. What else do you think they could have used to put the tent up?
- Look at pages 10 and 11. How do you think the kids are feeling? Why do you think that?
- Look at pages 12 and 13. Why do you think the sacks had a horrible smell?
- Look at pages 14 and 15. What else do you think the kids could have done to solve the problem?

EXPLORING LANGUAGE

Terminology
Author and illustrator credits, ISBN number

Vocabulary
Clarify: camping, sleeping bags, headphones, tent, pegs, sacks
Singular/Plural: bag/bags, sack/sacks, peg/pegs
Homonyms: their/there, too/to/two

Print Conventions
Apostrophes – contractions (let's, we'll, didn't, he's); ellipsis, dash

Phonological Patterns
Focus on short and long vowels **u** (b**u**mping, p**u**t, m**u**st, tr**u**ck, **u**se)
Discuss suffixes and base words (fall**en**, stopp**ed,** snor**ing**)